SPARROWS DON'T DROP
CANDY WRAPPERS

SPARROWS

DON'T DROP
CANDY WRAPPERS

By Margaret Gabel
Illustrated by Susan Perl

DODD, MEAD & COMPANY
NEW YORK

For John Wesley Booker III,
John McIlwain, Jr.,
Rocco Malcé,
and an earthful of other young people,
with the hope they'll grow up
in a cleaner, happier world

"One man can make a difference,
and every man should try."
—*John Kennedy*

Sparrows don't drop candy wrappers. Beavers build no billboards. Trees don't shed tin cans. Dolphins don't dump chemicals into the water. Bears don't belch carbon monoxide. And butterflies need no pesticides.

How did the air, the water, and the earth become so polluted that our sources of food, our lungs, and our life expectancy are eroding?

We have met the enemy, and he is us, as Pogo has pointed out.

And *us* means you and me, not *them*—not industry or big business, but all of *us* who want, ask for, use up, and discard the things that must be stripped from the earth, the air, and the oceans.

If our world is a foul-smelling, unhealthy eyesore, it is we who are to blame. We are the ones who must change it by being aware of what is harmful and of what contributes to the natural order that makes our world life-sustaining.

Ecology, the study of the relationships between living things and their environment, is not simply another specialized science or a momentary fad. According to a prominent biologist, "The first law of ecology is that every thing is related to everything else." We must remember that none of our natural resources is unlimited. Damage to any of them has far-reaching effects on all life.

Nobody *likes* dirty streets, littered beaches, polluted air, spoiled countryside, or filthy streams. But each of us contributes to the mess every day by being wasteful, by not thinking, by being unaware of the dangers, by shifting the blame to others.

It will require all of us—thinking, caring, being aware, and doing something about it daily— to repair the damage. It can be done if we act instead of waiting for other people to do something.

We can start with simple things.

TREES DON'T SHED TIN CANS

Aboard one of the U.S. Navy's deep submersible craft, fifty miles off the coast of San Diego, and 2,450 feet down, Admiral R. J. Galanson, chief of naval wonders, peered through the portholes to view an undersea world no man had ever seen. The first thing he spotted, only two feet away on the ocean floor, was an empty beer can.

—LESLIE ROBINSON
NEBRASKA STATE SENATE

Getting rid of waste is a constantly expanding problem, for disposal is often accomplished by means that increase air and water pollution. Waste is burned, and the smoke pollutes the air. Or it is dumped into the sea, and the water becomes polluted. Two conditions make this a bigger problem than ever before: There are now more of us in the world to discard wastes, and there is more clutter involved in the goods we use.

Fancy, eye-catching packages are big offenders. Often a product the size of a nail brush will be encased in a foot of cardboard and cellophane. Try to buy products that come without this unnecessary packaging. Somewhere along the line a tree was destroyed, a squirrel's home was toppled, birds' nests were crushed, and all the minute forest life dependent on these things was disrupted —all to provide a nail brush with a pink and orange display box.

Dramatize your opposition to excess packaging by removing the item from its container at the check-out counter. Explain why you are doing this. Stores will soon get the message and pass it along to manufacturers.

Buy items in containers that decompose readily. Aluminum does not. Plastic does not. Pasteboard, cardboard, and paper are better.

Buy returnable bottles instead of indestructible aluminum cans. (The old-fashioned tin ones used to rust at least.) Collect and return all returnable bottles and get the money for them. Don't patronize stores that have a policy of not selling returnables. Write to the manufacturer and request a return to returnables.

Some aluminum companies have established reclamation centers for their used cans. Find out if there's one near you. If so, collect aluminum cans and return them. The companies pay ten cents per pound (there are about twenty twelve-ounce beverage cans in a pound). If there isn't a reclamation center close by, try to interest a civic group in providing transportation to the nearest one at certain times of the year. Tell them that you and a friend will collect and store the cans between trips. (Does anyone have an empty corner in his cellar or garage? If not, ask a local businessman to donate storage space.)

Take metal hangers back to the cleaners if you don't need them. Throwing them away will just create more garbage. And don't accept those plastic shrouds cleaners put over clothes.

Protesting pollution? Don't wear indestructible metal buttons to say so.

Talk back to people who send out junk mail. Return the mail to the sender in his own prepaid envelope, without ordering his product. Or save up a bundle from the same source and return it in one big problem package, to show the sender what you had to cope with.

Save, wash, and reuse those unavoidable plastic bags that everything comes in.

If you buy something small enough for pocket or purse, don't accept a bag for it. And when you shop for more than a single item, consolidate your purchases in one bag—maybe even a net bag you've brought along yourself.

Consider the total life cycle of any purchase. What went into its making? How will it be disposed of when you're through with it?

Reusing materials—recycling—is an important concept. Every reclaimed pound of paper, or aluminum, or iron is a pound less solid waste in our environment, as well as a pound less that has to be stripped from the earth for replacement. The dump, the incinerator, the garbage scow all contribute to pollution. Recycling doesn't. So if a thing—*any* thing—is reusable or returnable, reuse or return it. Don't contribute to the mountains of garbage.

If you can't use something, call your local thrift shop. Someone can probably use what you're throwing away.

Stop littering now. And tell everybody you see dropping papers and trash on the streets to *stop, now.* Put that candy wrapper in your pocket until you find a trash can. And if your neighborhood is short of public trash cans, write the mayor and tell him so. Or raise the money to buy a trash can by cashing in aluminum cans and returnable bottles.

Consider how much it costs your town to clean up litter and garbage.

If you are lucky enough to be well provided for, ask relatives and friends to donate to a conservation cause at Christmas time or on your birthday—instead of giving you more scarves and slippers you don't need.

Keep your sidewalk swept, your lawn tidy. If the street cleaner doesn't come in close enough, clean the gutter yourself. Organize the neighbors for a block cleaning party, or a tree planting day.

If you live in the city, be sure to curb your dog so that people can walk on the sidewalks without running an obstacle course. Don't be afraid to speak to dog owners who are not leading their animals to the curb or whose dogs use the base of a tree. Tell them the law requires curbing dogs, and that dog urine corrodes the tree bark and injures the tree. Be polite but firm. If you don't have a dog and you live in the city, think twice about getting one. A turtle, a cat, or a gerbil won't add to the mess of the streets.

Do you have a favorite picnic or camping spot? Don't leave trash to spoil it. Clean up after yourself, and after others if they've left a mess.

If there is a vacant lot or unused space in your neighborhood, help make it a joy instead of an eyesore. Approach the owner for permission; then organize your friends to clean it up and keep it clean. Or do it by yourself. Plant something. It doesn't take the government to make a park. All it takes are a few people who care.

The more green things around you, the better the air you breathe, because plants produce oxygen in the process of photosynthesis. Plant a tree, or plant a window box. If you don't have plants of your own, adopt some. Protect and take care of growing things in the parks and along the streets or roads.

If you live in the city, take an interest in the
trees planted along your block. If they look dry,
loosen the packed earth at their base and give
them a pail of water. Maybe two pails. Ask a
neighbor for help.

One man saved an entire vest pocket park. He saw twenty-five newly planted trees perishing during a dry spell, and he called the city parks department every day until a water truck came to water them.

Use live Christmas trees instead of amputated ones, and plant them after the holiday. If you live in the city, give a country friend your tree, or keep it in a pot in your living room. Do you want to give someone a special birthday or anniversary gift? Plant a tree in his honor.

Stone cemetery markers aren't as beautiful as trees. Consider a living memorial instead of cut flowers and a granite block.

When you plant a tree or flowers, fertilize the soil if need be. But try to use natural fertilizers. If you live in the country, start a compost heap of plant clippings and vegetable wastes. This decayed matter will make excellent fertilizer. When you must use chemical fertilizers, make sure they are worked deep into the soil so that rain runoff won't wash pollutants into nearby waterways.

Planned gardens are beautiful, but so are natural ones. If you don't want to cultivate a garden, let nature do it. Don't be scornful of weeds; don't destroy them. Many are attractive, and all contribute to the life cycle of some organism.

There's another way to be kind to trees: Don't waste the paper products that are made from them. If you do you are encouraging lumberers and manufacturers to desecrate more forests.

Use cloth napkins and towels instead of paper ones.

Use glasses and china plates instead of paper cups and plates.

Don't buy anything that is 90 percent fancy packaging.

Share your newspaper and magazine subscriptions.

Call your local newspaper and find out about returning old papers for recycling and reuse.

Use a postcard instead of paper and envelope for short messages.

Keep a blackboard instead of a pad by your telephone for messages.

Don't waste paper at school or at work. If part of a page is spoiled, cut up the rest for notepaper.

Again, remember that all life is part of an interrelated pattern. Herbicides—the chemicals used to control unwanted plants—may upset that pattern and cause more harm than good. Birds and animals feed on those plants and are affected by the poisons. If your town uses herbicides to control roadside vegetation, write your mayor and ask questions.

Work to keep informed on all these problems and pass along your knowledge and ideas to other people. Post notices on the bulletin board at school or at your job. Write a letter to the editor of your town newspaper. Talk to your friends and neighbors about ways to improve your community ecologically. Don't be shy about criticizing offenders. Pollution is too grave a danger.

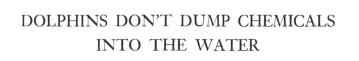

DOLPHINS DON'T DUMP CHEMICALS INTO THE WATER

Of all our natural resources, water has become the most precious . . . most of the world's population is either experiencing or is threatened with critical shortages. . . . Water must be thought of in terms of the chains of life it supports—from the small-as-dust green cells of the drifting plant plankton, through the minute water fleas to the fishes that strain plankton from the water and are in turn eaten by other fishes or birds, minks, raccoons—in an endless cyclic transfer of materials from life to life. We know that the necessary minerals in the water are so passed from link to link of the food chains. Can we suppose that poisons we introduce into water will not also enter these cycles of nature?

—RACHEL CARSON
Silent Spring

Plankton, a tiny ocean plant, produces most of the oxygen that sustains all sea life. Pollution of our oceans and their contributory waterways is a grave threat to these life-giving plants. Take a few steps toward reducing water pollution and conserving the water we have. Remember that no natural resource—including water—is unlimited.

Don't flush anything down the toilet or wash anything down the drain that can be disposed of elsewhere. For example, save cooking fats in a jar. (You'll have suet for the birds.) Ask smokers not to flush away filter tips; they don't disintegrate. If you live in the country, add those coffee grounds, tea leaves, and all such vegetable wastes to your compost heap.

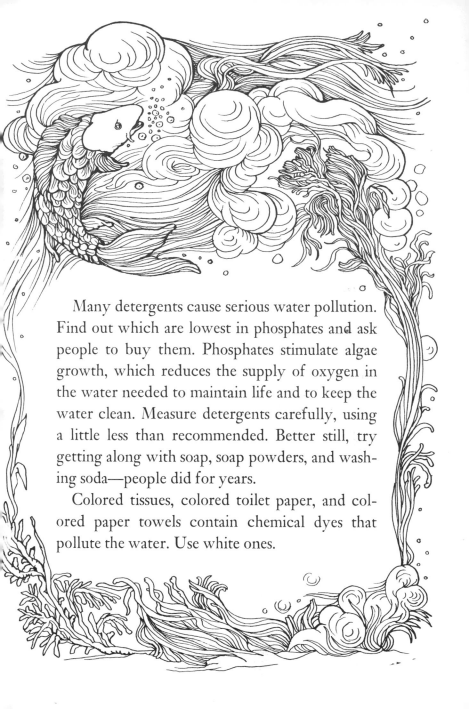

Many detergents cause serious water pollution. Find out which are lowest in phosphates and ask people to buy them. Phosphates stimulate algae growth, which reduces the supply of oxygen in the water needed to maintain life and to keep the water clean. Measure detergents carefully, using a little less than recommended. Better still, try getting along with soap, soap powders, and washing soda—people did for years.

Colored tissues, colored toilet paper, and colored paper towels contain chemical dyes that pollute the water. Use white ones.

Don't waste water. Repair leaky faucets and pipes. Don't leave the water running while you brush your teeth. Don't wash dishes under running water. Don't fill the tub to the top. Or take a shower instead of a bath; it requires less water. For cold drinking water, keep a jug in the refrigerator.

Pick up trash and debris along beaches and river banks. Don't hesitate to be conspicuous. Others will learn or take courage from your example.

If you know of a business that dumps dyes, chemicals, or other wastes into your local river or stream, write to the president of that company and suggest his firm improve its method of disposal. Write to your local newspaper and point out the dangers of such pollution. Write to your mayor and local government officials. And if nothing happens, letter some signs and go picket the plant with your friends.

Does your town have a municipal sewage treatment plant? If not, is it dumping untreated wastes into the waterways? If it has such a plant, is the operation equipped to deal with the complex new chemical pollutants?

Demand for water is constantly increasing. The dependable supply of fresh water is not. Rivers and streams have an amazing ability to purify themselves, but our rate of pollution is exceeding their rate of purification.

BEARS DON'T BELCH CARBON MONOXIDE

Motor vehicles produce more than half the air pollution in this country. Take a small step toward curbing this breathtaking problem.

If you don't really need a car, find some other way to get around. Ride a bike. Walk. Use public transportation.

Promote a back-to-biking movement, including action for more bike racks at school or work and safe bicycle paths.

Support legislation for better mass transit systems.

If you must use a car, share it with other riders; form a car pool. To quote the late Walter Reuther, president of the United Auto Workers: "It's asinine—I don't know a better word for it —to have hundreds of people all going to the same place at the same time for the same purpose and all of them dragging two tons of gadgets with them."

If an automobile is necessary, at least use lead-free gas. And why not buy a car with low horse-power and high mileage? There's no excuse for those luxury motels on wheels, spewing noxious fumes, taking *one* selfish person somewhere at the expense of all of us.

Remind motorists who complain about traffic jams that they are the problem. More highways will only mean less green countryside, and will not solve the problem.

At home, switch off those gadgets you don't need. The less power we use, the less we contribute to the need for building more power plants, which pollute both air and water.

Turn off the lights when you leave a room. Put low-wattage bulbs in lamps not used for reading. Do you really need an electric toothbrush? Or an electric can opener? Or electric hair curlers? Remember that air conditioners take an enormous amount of power; use them sparingly. In winter, set the thermostat a few degrees lower than usual (a cool room is healthier); wear a sweater.

When you see heavy black smoke coming from a chimney, find the building owner and have a talk. If that doesn't have any effect, report the offense to the proper city agency.

Remember that *all* smoke pollutes the air to some extent. And particularly dangerous is the hydrochloric acid given off by those soft plastic containers made of polyvinyl chloride used for such things as shampoo and household cleaners. Try not to buy them.

Publicity hurts polluters. Get in touch with
your town or school newspaper, pointing out
factories and business concerns that belch too
much smoke. Ask the editor to run a daily col-
umn about the problems. Ask your minister or
rabbi to speak up for God's green earth. Make it
your club project to attack some of the dangers.
Above all, be aware of sound ecological practices
in your daily life.

BUTTERFLIES NEED NO PESTICIDES

In the long run, man might be more successful biologically and find greater meaning to life if he tried to collaborate with natural forces instead of conquering them.

—RENÉ DUBOS
ROCKEFELLER UNIVERSITY

Widespread use of pesticides, especially in farming, has had repercussions that are still to be measured. The ripples of destruction caused by these products are ever widening; we simply *do not know* what the long-range effects will be. But the harm to all forms of life may be irreversible.

Some things in nature men think they can do without—certain bugs, for instance, or commercially valueless swamplands. It is unwise, however, to think that anything in nature—no matter how annoying—is dispensable.

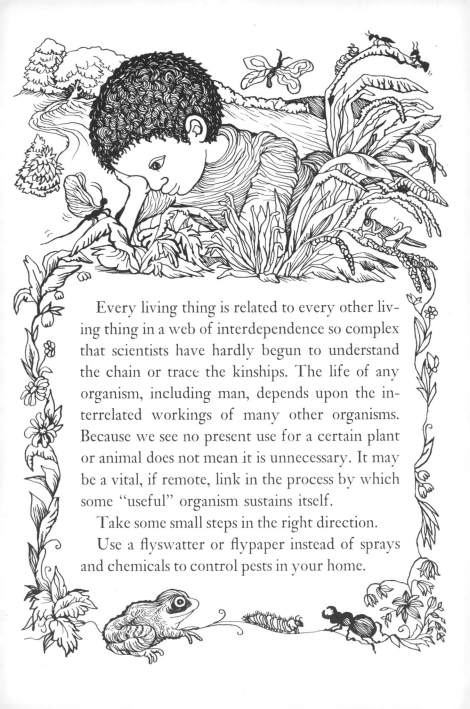

Every living thing is related to every other living thing in a web of interdependence so complex that scientists have hardly begun to understand the chain or trace the kinships. The life of any organism, including man, depends upon the interrelated workings of many other organisms. Because we see no present use for a certain plant or animal does not mean it is unnecessary. It may be a vital, if remote, link in the process by which some "useful" organism sustains itself.

Take some small steps in the right direction.

Use a flyswatter or flypaper instead of sprays and chemicals to control pests in your home.

Unless that spider, ant, or centipede poses a positive danger to you, let it live. It may be controlling something more obnoxious.

Ladybugs and praying mantises are excellent natural pest controls. Spare them. Encourage them.

Birds have always helped control insect populations. If your back yard is overrun with bugs, set up a birdbath and bird feeder to lure some helpers.

Don't plant just elms, only oak trees, or all maples. Vary the plants around you, thus discouraging an influx of parasites that feed on a particular species.

Attention to the natural growth in your area will suggest what kinds of plants thrive in your particular conditions. Don't try to force misfits. Concentrate on plants that do well naturally. There will be less need for fertilizers and more resistance to pests.

Here's an easy one: Don't buy fur coats or fur hats or fur rugs or alligator shoes or anything using the furs or skins of our vanishing wildlife. Express your disapproval to store owners who continue to stock the hides of endangered species. Some animal died for that fashion twaddle, and one day it may be the last of the species.

Twenty-two species of our wildlife are gone forever, and eighty await the end of their kind. The grizzly bear and wolf are near extinction. The whooping crane and ivory-billed woodpecker can easily go the way of the passenger pigeon unless wilderness areas are preserved for them. Support legislation for such areas. Write your congressmen.

The tiger population of India has decreased drastically from 40,000 tigers fifty years ago to 2,800 today, through overshooting, loss of habitat, and commercial demand for their skins.

In America, after years of spraying pesticides to kill insects, we have almost wiped out our national symbol—the bald eagle. Pesticides from the bird's food have accumulated in its tissues to the point of impairing reproduction.

Poisoning through pesticides and herbicides, loss of habitat caused by air and water pollution, and man's encroachment have destroyed much of our wildlife.

Find out which animals are "endangered" (you're on the list, by the way). And if you have friends who hunt, alert them to the possible extinction of certain species. Suggest hunting with a camera.

He prayeth best who loveth best
All things both great and small;
For the dear God, who loveth us,
He made and loveth all.

—S. T. COLERIDGE
Rime of the Ancient Mariner

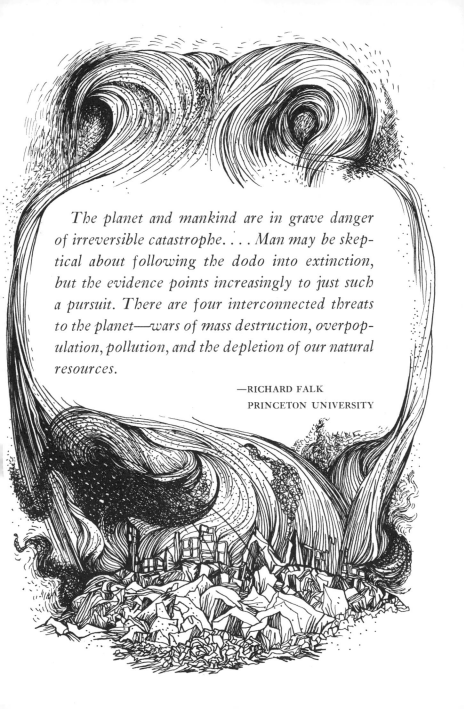

The planet and mankind are in grave danger of irreversible catastrophe. . . . Man may be skeptical about following the dodo into extinction, but the evidence points increasingly to just such a pursuit. There are four interconnected threats to the planet—wars of mass destruction, overpopulation, pollution, and the depletion of our natural resources.

—RICHARD FALK
PRINCETON UNIVERSITY

What is the point of all the flap about air, water, plants, animals, and so on?

Man. The quality of his life. That he be able to live in health, to breathe pure air, to enjoy the physical world and turn his enjoyment to learning and understanding. That he be taken off the list of endangered species.

Man is a great natural resource—and the most dangerous one.

Scientists agree that the earth cannot long support our rate of population growth. Big families are creating big problems everywhere. A family that limits its growth is helping everyone. Be proud of small families and of the people who are adoptive or foster parents rather than biological ones. Resist popular pressures that suggest everyone must have children. Some of us might be much happier and more useful simply helping and loving other people's children.

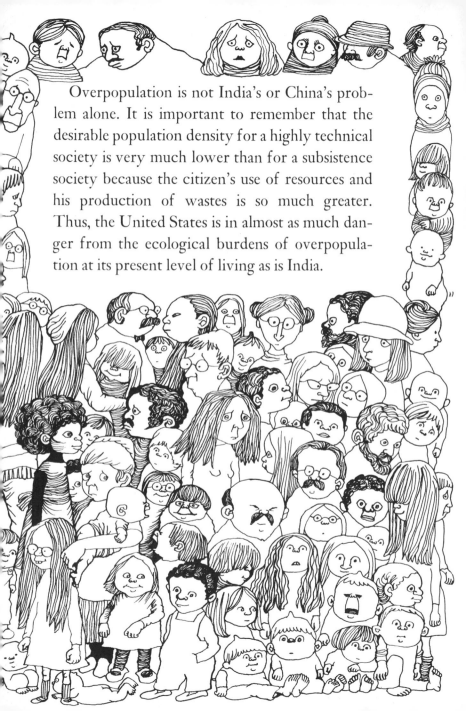

Overpopulation is not India's or China's problem alone. It is important to remember that the desirable population density for a highly technical society is very much lower than for a subsistence society because the citizen's use of resources and his production of wastes is so much greater. Thus, the United States is in almost as much danger from the ecological burdens of overpopulation at its present level of living as is India.

With only 6 percent of the world's population, Americans use up over half of the world's resources—and discard the rinds at an alarming rate. The average American uses more of the world's resources than any other human being. And he destroys these resources more rapidly, thereby contributing massively to the pollution of his own surroundings as well as of the whole world.

Perhaps our greatest value as one of the earth's natural resources will be the use of our unique minds to deal with the problems we have unleashed. We can recognize the dangers; we can keep ourselves informed; we can write to our newspapers and government officials to suggest or support solutions; we can remind people that our lives depend upon sane ecological practices. Above all, we can *act* each day, in many small but important ways, to reduce our share of the burden *homo sapiens* has inflicted upon the earth.

Consider yourself a valuable natural resource and act accordingly. Use your head, and take care of your body. Find out what foods are high in nutritional value, and avoid the junk foods. Health and energy are important; bulk and extra weight are not.

Many people don't yet recognize *noise* as a pollutant, but ask anyone who lives near an airport, in an area where there is construction going on, on a major highway, or on a street that is undergoing repair. Noise is a sneaky kind of pollution. Again, take a few small steps toward peace and quiet.

Ask drivers to use their horns only in emergencies, and to have their car mufflers checked frequently.

If you need a new garbage can, consider getting a heavy-duty plastic one. They make less noise. And the tops usually fit better, longer.

Keep radio, television, and phonograph volume low, especially after ten at night and before seven in the morning. Suggest that your local television and radio stations remind listeners to lower the volume at 10 P.M.

Mechanized recreation—snowmobiles, dune buggies, power boats, trail bikes, and jeeps—add to the water and air pollution as well as the noise pollution, and they take up a disproportionate amount of space in a world starving for the solace of wilderness. Snowmobiles, for instance, make ear-splitting noise, leave a wake of fumes, and intrude on the solitary skier and the snowshoe rabbit.

To live a decent human life you need those intangibles—clean air, clean water, grass—who can eat grass? You need it just the same. Trees, relationship to animals. Sounds sentimental, doesn't it? You forget those things and you're just a fraction of a man. And that's what we are out to do—to try to become whole men and women again.

—GEORGE WALD
HARVARD UNIVERSITY

Pollution endangers food and water and the air we breathe, threatening our health and life as physical creatures. But there is another, equally important part of man's relationship to his environment—his spiritual adjustment to the beauty or the ugliness of the world in which he lives.

Many pollution problems that are not immediately dangerous to physical health seriously affect our attitudes about life and people. Think of waking up to blue skies, robin songs, dewy grass —and then think of waking up to asphalt streets, smog, motor sounds. It is easy to see how our surroundings color our whole approach to life.

It is impossible to measure the spiritual aspect of the pollution problem, but it is still vitally important. The ugliness of our environment fosters an ugliness within us that is as far-reaching and destructive as what we are doing to the physical world.

The Lord God planted Man in a garden of delight, to dress it and to tend it. —Genesis

Tending the earth for beauty and health might be a way you'd like to spend your life. Think about that when it's time to change jobs or to decide how to earn your living. Earning a living might have a broader meaning for you than for those who do other work.

Whatever our business or way of life, an obligation to endure demands that we pay attention to the well-being of our natural world.

Every living thing—you, me, the cat, the sparrow, trees, butterflies—all of us need good air and pure water and enough food. The earth gives us air and food and water. It keeps us alive. Let's return the favor.

SUGGESTED READING

Rachel Carson, *Silent Spring*. New York: Crest.

Garrett De Bell, ed., *The Environmental Handbook*. New York: Ballantine.

William O. Douglas, *Wilderness Bill of Rights*. Boston: Little, Brown.

René Dubos, *So Human an Animal*. New York: Charles Scribner's Sons.

Paul Erlich, *The Population Bomb*. New York: Ballantine.

Joseph Wood Krutch, *The Great Chain of Life*. Boston: Houghton Mifflin.

Wesley Marx, *The Frail Ocean*. New York: Ballantine.

John G. Mitchell and Constance L. Stallings, eds., *Ecotactics:* The Sierra Club Handbook for Environmental Tactics. New York: Pocket Books.

National Staff of Environmental Action, eds., *Earth Day:* The Beginning. New York: Bantam Books.

Henry David Thoreau, *In Wildness Is the Preservation of the World*, edited by Eliot Porter. New York: Ballantine.